Draw

Draw SCIENCE FICTION

Written and illustrated by Granger Davis

Lowell 🏠 House
Juvenile
Los Angeles

CONTEMPORARY BOOKS
Chicago

Publisher: Jack Artenstein
Vice President, Juvenile Division: Elizabeth Amos
Director of Publishing Services: Rena Copperman
Editorial Director: Brenda Pope-Ostrow
Senior Editor: Amy Downing
Art Director: Lisa-Theresa Lenthall
Cover Illustration: Steve Feldman

ISBN: 1-56565-355-6

10 9 8 7 6 5 4 3 2 1

CONTENTS

DRAWING TIPS

This book shows you how to draw 22 out-of-this-world mutants, aliens, and other extraterrestrial life-forms, as well as the various space vehicles they use to charge around the galaxy. There are lots of different ways to draw, and you're about to learn quite a few of them. You'll also find some helpful hints throughout this book to help make your drawings the best they can be. But before you launch, here are some tips that every aspiring artist should know!

- Use a large sheet of paper and make your drawing fill up the space. That way, it's easy to see what you are doing, and it will give you plenty of room to add details.

- When you are blocking in large shapes, draw by moving your whole arm, not just your fingers or your wrist.

- Experiment with different kinds of lines: do a light line, then gradually bear down for a wider, darker one. You'll find that just by changing the thickness of a line, your whole picture will look different! Also, try groups of lines. You can draw all the lines in a group straight, crisscross, curved, or jagged.

- Remember that every artist has his or her own style. That's why the pictures you draw won't look exactly like the ones in the book. Instead, they'll reflect your own creative touch.

- Most of all, have fun!

WHAT YOU'LL NEED

PAPER
Many kinds of paper can be used for drawing, but some are better than others. For pencil drawing, avoid newsprint or rough papers because they don't erase well. Instead, use a large pad of bond paper (or a similar type). The paper doesn't have to be thick, but it should be uncoated, smooth, and cold pressed. You can find bond paper at an art store. If you are using ink, a dull-finished, coated paper works well.

PENCILS, CHARCOAL, AND PENS
A regular school pencil is fine for the drawings in this book, but try to use one with soft lead. Pencils with soft lead are labeled No. 2; No. 3 pencils have a hard lead. If you want a thicker lead, ask an art store clerk or your art teacher for an artist's drafting pencil.

Charcoal works well when you want a very black line. If you're just starting to draw with charcoal, use a charcoal pencil of medium to hard grade. With it, you will be able to rub in shadows, then erase certain areas to make highlights. Work with large pieces of paper, as charcoal is difficult to control in small drawings. And remember that charcoal smudges easily!

If you want a smooth, thin ink line, try a rolling-point or a fiber-point pen. Art stores and bigger stationery stores carry these in a variety of line widths and fun, bright colors.

ERASERS

An eraser is one of your most important tools! Besides removing unwanted lines and cleaning up smudges, erasers can be used to make highlights and textures. Get a soft plastic type (the white ones are good), or for very small areas, a gray kneaded eraser can be helpful. Try not to take off ink with an eraser because it will ruin the drawing paper. If you must take an ink line out of your picture, use liquid whiteout.

OTHER HANDY TOOLS

Facial tissues are helpful for creating soft shadows—just go over your pencil marks with a tissue, gently rubbing the area you want smoothed out.

A square of metal window screen is another tool that can be used to make shadows. Hold it just above your paper and rub a soft pencil lead across it. Then, using a tissue, rub the pencil shavings into the paper to make a smooth shadowed area in your picture. If you like, you can sharpen the edge of the shadow with your eraser.

You will also need a pencil sharpener, but if you don't have one, rub a small piece of sandpaper against the side of your pencil to keep the point sharp.

As you'll see with the creatures and cruising vehicles in this book, artists must use different drawing techniques to make their creations look smooth, rough, hairy, wet, and so on. Here are some useful techniques for giving your drawings the variety of looks you'll want.

HATCHING

Hatching is a group of short, straight lines used to create a texture or a shadow. When you curve the hatching lines, you create a rounded look. This is handy when texturing a creature's curved body parts or underside. When you draw the hatching lines close together, you create a dark shadow. For very light shading, draw the lines shorter, thinner, and farther apart.

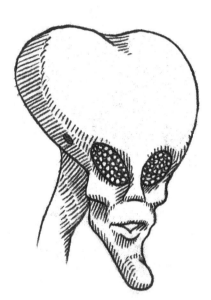

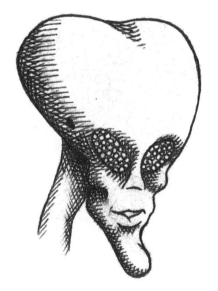

CROSS-HATCHING

This technique gives your alien a wrinkled, textured look. Start with an area of hatching, then crisscross it with a new set of lines. If you are drawing wrinkles on skin, make the lines a bit wobbly and uneven, just as creases in real skin would be. Take a look at the head of the Heavy-Headed Humanoid to see how cross-hatching creates a rough-skinned look. This is also a great technique to use for battle-damaged spaceships.

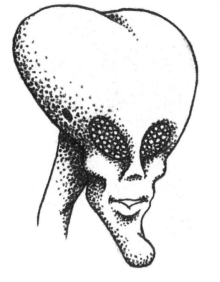

STIPPLE

When you want to give your drawing a different feel, try the stipple technique—and all you need are dots! This method works best with a pen, because unlike a pencil, a pen will make an even black dot by just touching the paper.

The stipple technique is very similar to the way photos are printed in newspapers and books. If you look through a magnifying glass at a picture in a newspaper, you will see very tiny dots. The smaller and farther apart the dots are, the lighter the area is. The larger and closer the dots are, the darker the area. In your drawings, you can make a shadow almost black just by placing your stipple dots close together.

SMOOTH TONE

By using the side of your pencil, you can create a smooth texture on your creature. This technique is also great for giving your spaceship a hi-tech, metallic look. Starting with the areas you want to be light, stroke the paper very lightly and evenly. Put a little bit more pressure on your pencil as you move to the sections you want to be darker. If you want a spot even smoother, go back and rub the pencil with a facial tissue, but rub gently! If you get smudges in areas you want to stay white, simply remove them with an eraser.

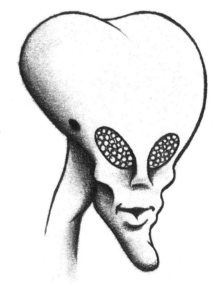

Now that you're armed with a few basic drawing tools and techniques, you're ready to get started on some otherworldly drawings.

Throughout this book, you'll find special Drawing Tips that will aid your progress. Last, at the back of the book are extra techniques and hints for using color, casting shadows, and placing creatures in a scene—in short, showing you how to make the most of your drawings.

This 25th-century scientist has been traveling the super-galactic information highway for so long, collecting so much data in his brain, his head is about to explode. That's enough to make any scientist go mad!

1 To begin creating this complex and crazy scientist, start with two very simple shapes. Draw a large circular shape for a giant cranium. Then sketch in an elongated oval shape with a squared-off bottom to create the body of the scientist.

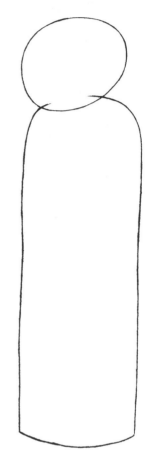

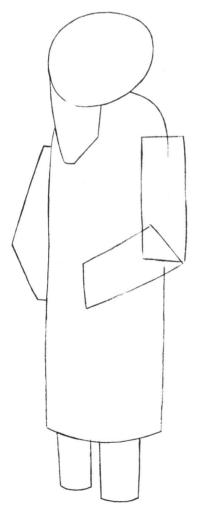

2 To the bottom of the rounded head, add a downward-pointing shape to create the outline of the scientist's face and chin. Then add his arms using rectangular shapes with straight edges and sharp corners. Extend two short cylindrical shapes from the bottom of the figure for his legs.

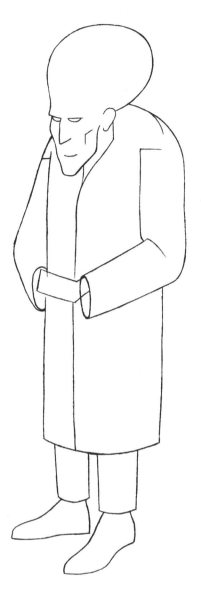

3 Begin to add facial detail by adding an ear, the eyes, nose, mouth, and cheekline. Add a small neckline, too. Draw a straight line down the middle of the body to create the opening of a lab coat. Round out the arms, especially at the elbows and shoulders to create a hunched-over look. Draw narrow ovals at the ends of the arms to transform those arms into sleeves. Add a rectangle that extends between the two sleeves—this will serve as part of the scientist's left hand. And since filling up that cranium is a never-ending job, be sure to give him a comfortable pair of lab shoes. Erase lines you no longer need, especially around the arms and head.

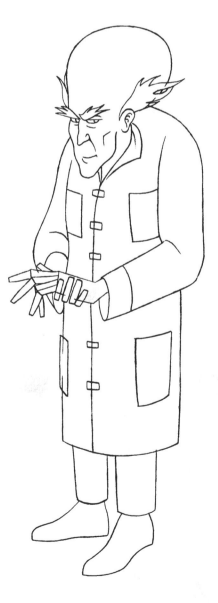

4 It's time to make your mad scientist come to life. Add detail to his face, and draw in flamelike hair features around his temple and above his eyes. Complete his collar, draw four pockets, and add small rectangular snaps down the middle of his lab coat. Then create crazy fingers by drawing long thin rectangles extending beyond the rectangle you drew between the sleeves in Step 3.

5 Draw hints of pulsating veins on the top of your scientist's head. Continue to detail his hair and eyebrows. Work carefully on the scientist's hands to round out the fingers, and add long sharp fingernails. Erase any excess marks in the hands.

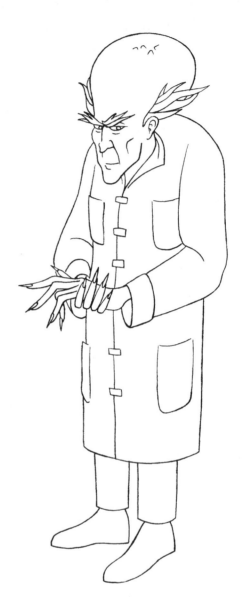

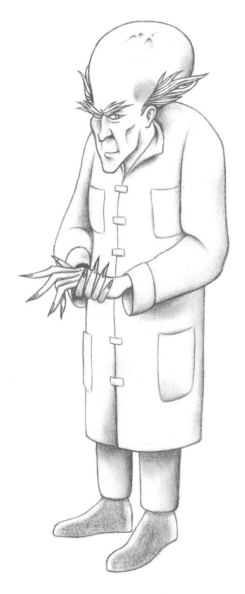

6 To complete your mad, mad scientist, add a few more lines in the hair, and color in the lab shoes using stippling. Lightly shade his coat, pants, and head as you wish.

Drawing Tip: Notice how careful use of relatively dark smooth-tone shading can give you some extraordinary results. Suddenly, the mad scientist has a more menacing look with the darkened areas in his face and hands. His cranium looks spherical instead of just rounded, and his temples have caved in!

This top-of-the-line spaceship fighter is armed with lasers, torpedoes, an invisible protective shield, and many other gadgets space pilots love. With its slick, compact design, it can maneuver its way through any asteroid field, not to mention a fleet of enemy battle cruisers!

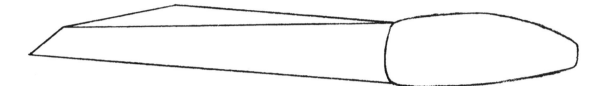

1   Draw a squarish, horizontal oval shape for the nose of the fighter. Sketch three straight lines extending back from the oval shape, with the bottom line extending out the farthest, then the center line, and finally, the shortest line on top. Connect the three lines with diagonal lines as shown.

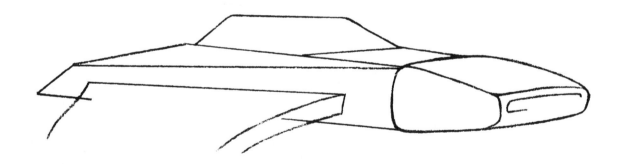

2   Toward the nose of the vehicle, add a flattened diamond shape that connects the nose with the top of the vehicle. Just to the left of that, add a raised cockpit for the pilots to sit in. Then begin to draw the right wing, using downward sloping lines and leaving the outer end of the wing open. Begin to add additional lines to the nose to create a more three-dimensional appearance, as well as an artillery window to the front end of the ship's nose.

3 Complete the right wing by adding a torpedo pod. Do the same on the far side to suggest a left wing (notice that the torpedo pod is only partially shown). Add window detail in the cockpit, and include two narrow missile barrels in the artillery window. Add two tail fin supports on the end of the fighter, with two small cylindrical engines above them.

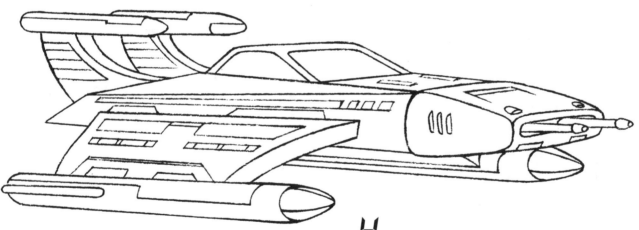

4 Now that your basic outline for the fighter is complete, it's time to add detail. Start with the tail fin supports and engines, adding horizontal lines as shown. Detail the right wing and the two torpedo pods, creating a launch hatch at the front end of both. Add a series of small boxed vents and lines on the body and nose of the vehicle, as well as two small headlights.

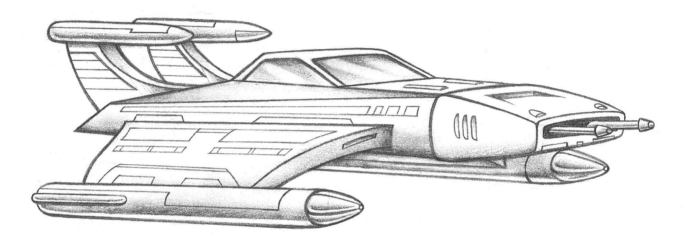

5 Give your Interplanetary Fighter sleek lines by lightly shading around the edges. Shading on the sides of the engines and torpedo pods, and on the underside of the nose and body, will create a rounded appearance. Darken the artillery windows around the missile barrels.

Drawing Tip: When it comes to drawing reflective glass windows, your eraser is your best tool. Start by lightly shading the whole window, then erase any areas you want highlighted. These areas will appear to be reflecting light.

This freaky creature makes an awesome pet, and it never gets lost because with so many eyes, it always knows where it's going!

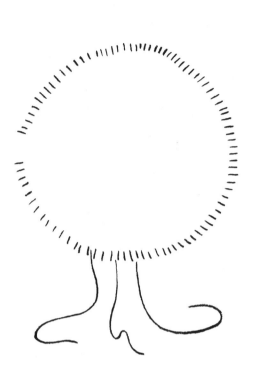

1 To start, draw a circle of short hairlike lines spaced close together. Leave a small space on the left side. Then draw three evenly spaced lines curling down and away from the circle for the creature's tentacle legs.

2 Draw three circles for the gigantic eyes, one just inside the hairy body, and the other two above and outside. Now connect each eye to the top of the body with a single curving line. As for the body, sketch in another hairy circle just inside the first one, using short hatch lines a bit more widely spaced. Draw three more evenly spaced lines around the tentacles to complete the Alien Ball Pet's slimy legs.

3 Now give those eyeballs some eyelids, as well as a small iris. Notice how the eye on the creature's left is ignoring you and looking sideways. Add thickness to the three eyestalks with additional lines. Continue drawing the short hairs, spaced more and more widely apart as you get closer to the center of the body. Erase unneeded lines around the eyeballs.

4 For this particular creature, you will add two kinds of detail: smooth-tone shading and hatching. Add smooth tones around the eyestalks and leg tentacles to give a smooth, almost moist look. For the fluffed-out hairy body, continue to fill in the surface with short hairs. Around the bottom of the creature, add thick, darker shadows as shown.

Drawing Tip: To give your pet's hair a short and spiky look, be sure to keep your pencil sharpened as you draw in the lines. When your drawing tool starts to get the slightest bit dull, sharpen it again!

Some of the terrain found on the outer planets of the galaxy is so desolate and harsh, the only way to traverse it is by Alien-Biped Transporter. The lizard creature's one drawback? It eats Alien Ball Pets for breakfast!

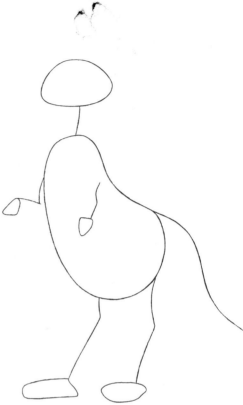

1 Your creation of this two-legged alien begins with a slightly flattened oval shape for the head. The body of the Alien-Biped Transporter is shaped very much like a pear. Draw it next. Then sketch in a short straight line connecting the head and body. Attach short squiggly arms with triangular hands. Then add a long curvy tail. Finally, stand your creature on two large feet, attached to jointed legs.

2 Now start to fill out the transporter's powerful body and limbs. Thicken the neck, arms, tail, and legs, drawing slightly curved lines around the thin sketch lines you drew in Step 1. To create claws, extend three small circular shapes from each hand and two from each foot. Then add flat oval eyes, as well as an elephantlike snout. Erase any extra lines, especially the skeletal lines from Step 1 that you no longer need.

3 It's time to begin detailing your alien. Add sharp curving horns to either side of its snout, as well as small ridges above and below each eye. Create a saddle that rests on the back of the creature and is anchored to belts that stretch around its neck and belly. Transform the small circular shapes you drew in Step 2 into fierce-looking claws. Add two small, hooked claws on the back of its feet. Erase all unneeded lines in the feet, hands, body, and head.

4 Add hatch lines here and there over its body to create the rubbery texture of its skin. Then add small circles to various parts of its body for scales. Detail the saddle and belts. Don't forget to add the saddle's two small handles (one is almost completely hidden).

5 Does the transporter look alien enough for you yet? If it doesn't, don't worry. This final step will make your Alien-Biped look out of this world! Continue adding small hatch lines around the body. Shade the rounded edges of its body and tail, as well as the saddle and belts. Be sure to finish the biped's eyes so it can transport you safely!

The Galactic Bounty Hunter of the future is the police officer of today, fighting for the safety and protection of all space beings. A bounty hunter will go to even the distant reaches of the galaxy to track down Space Pirates and other dangerous criminals.

1 Begin by creating the basic outline of the Galactic Bounty Hunter. First draw the helmet-covered head, making sure the points coming out of the helmet are sharp. Next create a downward semicircle, which is actually the top of the head. Below that, draw the large chest. Make sure it slightly overlaps the bottom of the helmet. Then attach two thin lines for the arms and add blocks for hands. Create the skeleton of the Bounty Hunter's legs by drawing lines below the body. The hunter is in a lunge stance, so his left leg should be bent and his right leg should be extended straight. Be sure to attach feet shapes to the legs. Add small cross lines at the knees, elbows, and neck.

2 Complete his helmet by connecting the two spikes with a semicircle, and adding an eye visor and mouthpiece. Now add two odd-shaped circles to the top of the body to create shoulder armor. Using the guidelines to direct you, fill out the Galactic Bounty Hunter's waist, arms, and legs.
Add in finger shapes as shown. And don't forget to draw the rectangular laser gun in his left hand.

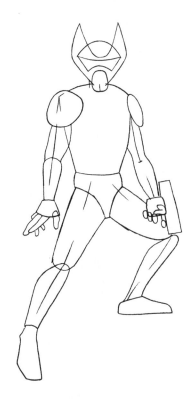

3 Erase any excess lines throughout his body and head. Add small rectangular slits to his mouthpiece. Create chest armor that has a muscled appearance to it. Add an ammunition belt over his right shoulder, as well as a belt around his waist. Continue to create the rest of his laser-proof armor, particularly on his shins, left thigh, and right arm. Notice that the hunter has a second gun in a holster that's strapped to him around his right thigh. Add that now. Also sketch in more detail on the blaster, and add small knuckle protectors on the right hand. Indicate a smaller ammunition storage compartment on the hunter's inner left thigh. Finally, turn the feet into shoes by simply adding a thin sole line.

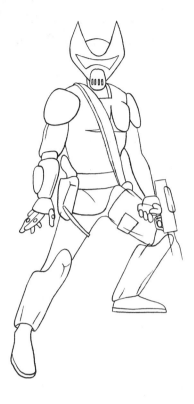

4 Next detail the ammo belt and storage compartment with straight lines. Add joints to the armored waist belt. Then add lines to the unprotected areas on his neck, arms, legs, and fingers. These lines make up a special super-flexible material that's virtually indestructible. Add a small rocket launcher to the top of his right forearm for some added firepower—and don't forget to include the control buttons! Complete the blaster. Erase unneeded lines in the armor, and add the small buttons on his right shin (the function of which is top secret).

5 Complete your Galactic Bounty Hunter with shading throughout. Darken the holes on the mouthpiece. With your eraser, highlight the front edges of the legs and right arm and shoulder. Create two highlight streaks in the visor to make it look like reflective glass.

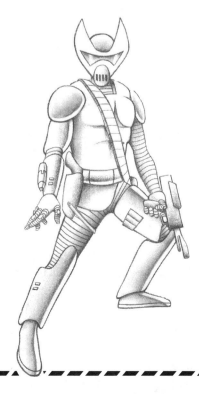

An honored warrior, this Galactic Gladiator Beast fights against other gladiators in the Beast League Games. No humans are allowed to play in the games—much too dangerous!

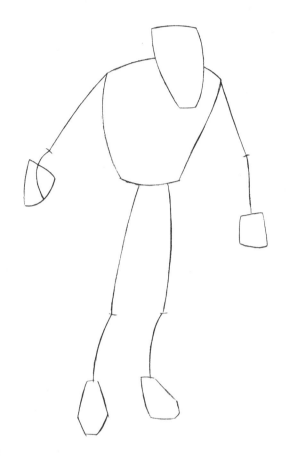

1 Begin with the head and large square-shaped body. Sketch in guidelines for the arms and legs, and add small shapes for the four paws. Add small cross lines to mark the joints at the elbows and knees.

2 Draw in slightly pointed ears and basic facial details, including the eyes, nose bridge, and snout. Sketch in oval shapes for the shoulder armor and smaller round shapes for the knee areas. Draw in curved lines on either side of the guidelines to fill out the arms and legs. Notice how large and jutting the calves are. Sketch in four small rounded square shapes to form fingers on the creature's right hand. Repeat these shapes on the feet for all eight toes. For the left hand, draw a ball and cone shape, which will serve as the beast's handy telegalactic outerspace communicator club.

Drawing Tip: For a different look, draw the Galactic Gladiator Beast with black pens, using a thin-line one for the shading and finer hair, and a thicker one for the shoulder plates and belt.

3 Soften and round out lines on the ears and face. With a few simple curved lines, draw the chest armor, with the appropriate areas falling under the shoulder plates. Draw small square bands to connect the shoulder and breast plates. Sketch in the belt and pants. On the creature's left hand, draw in small finger shapes holding the communicator club. Add a bit more detail to the device. Erase unneeded lines in the legs, arms, and head, and around the fingers and toes. Begin to add short hair lines along the arms, stomach area, paws, and feet. Add small claws, too. Begin drawing the Beast Alien's wicked tail, using a curved line as shown. The three forklike spikes at the end of the tail come in handy at the games.

4 Continue detailing with hair on the face, body, and limbs. Finish the hairy tail. With solid lines, detail the communicator club, the belt, and the shoulder and chest armor. Add some sharpness to the claws, then erase the unneeded lines in the toes, tail, and torso.

5 Your Galactic Gladiator is almost complete. All you need to do is add shading where shown. Extra-heavy shading on the armor will make it look thick and heavy. Add additional hair around the body, head, and tail.

With its six legs, sharp fangs, whiplike tail, and sleek body structure, this futuristic alien dog is more wild animal than tame pet. So don't get too close!

1 First block out the basic head and body shape of the animal. Sketch in single lines for the legs, and at the base of each one, draw in a small rounded foot shape. Don't forget to add in the curved tail line.

2 Next draw in two large curving triangles at the top of the head. These will become the creature's webbed ears. Begin to add simple facial details. On either side of the skeletal leg lines, begin sketching in loose short hairs to suggest thickness in the legs. Add three small toe ovals on each foot. The feet that fall behind the foreground legs need not be fully drawn since they will be partly hidden in the final drawing. Add another curving tail line, parallel to the first, to complete the thickness of the tail.

3 Continue to add detail to the face, ears, and tail. Add hair around the feet and along the underside of the Canine Creature. Erase the unneeded lines around the body, legs, and paws.

4 Finally, add heavy shading to the ears, mouth, and snout. Draw in an eyeball, and add detail to the tail. Continue adding thicker hairs around the body and face as desired.

Drawing Tip: One very effective method for creating shading is to softly move your pencil in short-to medium-length strokes that are very close together. If you like, try overlapping the lines.

ANTIGRAVITY SERVO-ROBOT

The latest in service-oriented technology, the Antigravity Servo-Robot cooks, cleans, vacuums, makes the beds, and will fetch an ice-cold glass of lemonade at your command. Oh, yeah, its microprocessors can handle 6.2 gigavolts of energy!

1 Begin with two half-egg shapes, the smaller, more rounded one on top, and the longer shape curved down to a point. Add a small circle to the base of your Servo-Robot.

2 Draw a wide ring around the area where the two halves meet. Lightly draw a pair of curving horizontal lines across the center of the top shape as guidelines for the "eyes." In between these guidelines and the ring, draw an upward-curving line to suggest the mouth. Next sketch in two lines for the arms, which should be holding a tray, suggested by a four-sided shape. A small rounded triangle forms the hand on the robot's right arm. Erase the unneeded lines inside the base circle.

3 Next add the small eyes between the guidelines. Draw another curving line parallel to the mouth line drawn in Step 2. Another curving ring line just under the first will give the ring a narrow side edge. Fill in the arms with additional lines as shown. Begin to sketch in the fingers and thumbs of the robot with small rectangles and circles. Don't forget to draw the left thumb holding the tray! Complete this tray by sketching in four lines parallel to the ones already drawn. Add the robot's brain center, which appears on its chest. On the back of its head, sketch in the tip of its erg-recepticalis (its power portal).

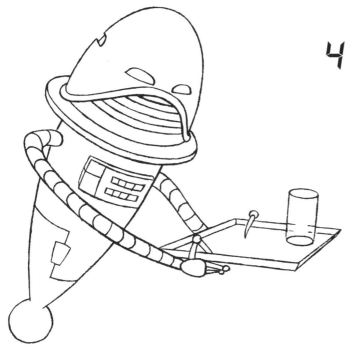

4 Fill in the mouth area with several lines, and add a series of small curved lines up and down the length of the arms. Detail the control panel on the Servo-Robot's chest. The base of the robot is actually a hinged panel. Fill in the joint lines of this panel, and the hinge, too. Add a glass on the tray—two horizontal squished ovals, connected with two vertical lines.

5 To give your robot a smooth metallic look, shade the robot as shown, using the side of a dark pencil. Remember to shade in the tray, as well as fill the glass with your favorite beverage. Now your Antigravity Servo-Robot's wish is to fulfill your every command!

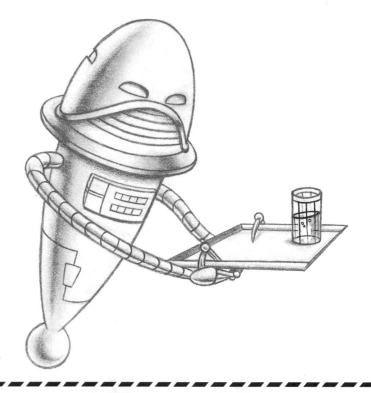

Whether this tough and cool Interstellar Soldier is an alien or a human in robot's clothing we may never know. But he is dedicated to protecting his quadrant of the galaxy and keeping it safe for all inhabitants.

1 Begin with the large chest area, then add an oval-shaped head. Lightly sketch in guidelines for the arms, legs, and neck. Draw in the soldier's right hand, both feet, and a single short line for the soldier's left hand. Establish the knee joints by drawing in two cross lines.

2 Next draw a larger oval shape around the head to indicate the helmet. Use additional oval shapes to define the shoulder, elbow, and knee armor plates. The rest of the body should be filled out, building from the skeletal guidelines. Pay special attention to the torso and pelvis areas. Suggest the automatic blaze stunner with a simple rectangular shape, held in the soldier's hands. Now add the finger shapes as shown.

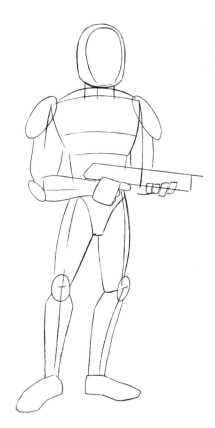

3 Now it's time to begin the heavy-duty armor. Add a muscular chest plate, as well as rounded plates on the upper arms, fronts and backs of the thighs, and shins. Add the large boots, too, which connect to the shin plates. Continue to detail the blaze stunner with a handle, trigger, and nose. Finally, add smaller shapes to the head area, suggesting an ear, facial visor, and mouth opening. Erase the guidelines added earlier.

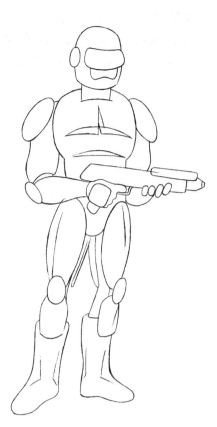

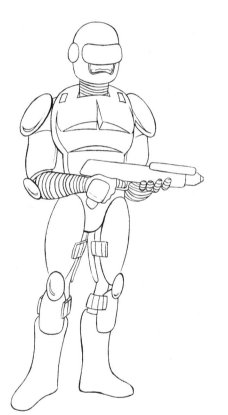

4 Draw in details around the mouth area, below the visor. On the neck, forearms, and fingers, add a protective material made of thin stripes. Then add the straps that hold the thigh and shin plates in place (notice that the shin straps reach all the way around the calf). For additional detail, add in a small square near each shoulder. Erase unnecessary lines in the arms, legs, and feet.

5 To prepare your Interstellar Soldier for battle, shade him from the bottom of his boots to the top of his armored helmet. Next to the darkest shading, use your eraser to create stark areas of highlight for a polished metal look.

Robot + Humanoid = Ro-Boid. This wonder of microcircuitry may think, act, and feel like a person, but its looks set it apart from the human race . . . *far* apart.

1 Because it's a *humanoid* robot, Ro-Boid's body is shaped very much like, well, a human body. Begin your creation by drawing the outline of the head. It should be shaped similar to a human skull that is facing slightly to the side. Next, draw the four-sided chest with slightly curved lines. Add guidelines for the arms and small blocks for the hands. Draw two more lines for the legs, marking the neck and knees with small cross lines. Finally, create the outline of the robot's mechanical feet, with one foot facing forward and the other foot facing sideways.

2 Create the robot's oval ear, and add the neck. Draw circles for the shoulders, with the left shoulder partially hidden, and fill out the arms. Use curved lines to create wrists, then draw in the robot's pelvis. Be sure to leave some space at the waist. Draw circles for the knees and partial circles for the ankles, then fill in the lower legs.

Drawing Tip: Combine very dark shading with lighter shading to create the most three-dimensional character possible. You may even want to use different types of pencils, such as the No. 2 pencil for the darker sections and No. 3 for lighter areas.

3 It's now time to give Ro-Boid some of its mechanical robotic features, such as its eyes and an open mouth. Attach metal rectangular fingers to its hands with knuckles made of metal circles. Draw thick curving cables to attach the hips to the chest, and sketch in a rounded shape in the space at the waist. Complete the robot's legs by filling in the thighs and attaching them to the hips with two round partially shown sockets.

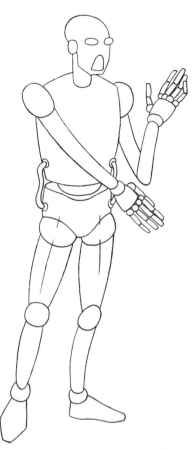

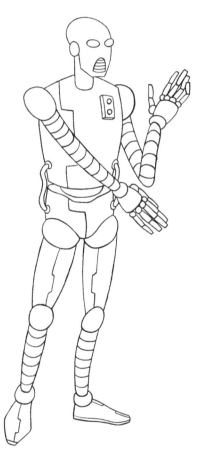

4 Sketch in metallic plates on its mouth, arms, and legs by drawing horizontal lines. Be sure to draw the robot's control panel on the top of its chest. If you don't, you'll have no way to control your robot, and who knows what kind of trouble it could get into! Then add a variety of metal seams on its chest, hips, legs, and feet.

5 To give Ro-Boid a shiny-smooth finish, shade it in as shown. Note the heavier shading across the chest and down the sides and legs. By contrast, other areas are highlighted.

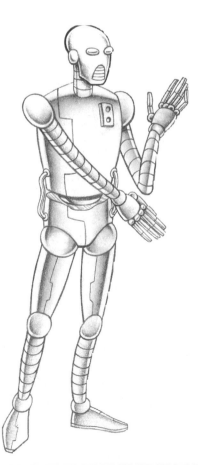

This futuristic floating vehicle eliminates the need for highways and gasoline. Simply pump it full with specially formulated techno-fuel . . . and go!

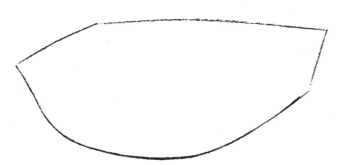

1 Begin with this basic wide shape. Make sure to curve the bottom line up to meet the other, straighter lines.

2 Add two cylinder engine shapes at the left and right sides of the main body. Draw a line running through the back of the vehicle to create a boxlike cockpit. Be sure to leave the front end of the cockpit open.

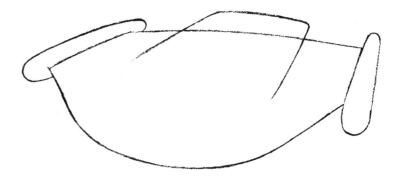

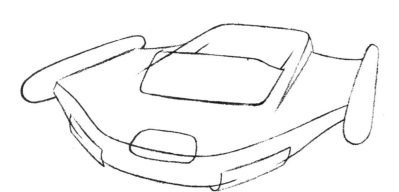

3 Add a rectangular curving window, and detail the sides of the cockpit. To the front end of the body, add a second curved line parallel to the first to give a three-dimensional shape to the main body of the speeder. Sketch in a small squarish nose trunk, and indicate curved rectangular bumper shapes to the left and right of this trunk.

4 Add two headlights and details on the the trunk space, and finish the bumpers. Clearly define the windshield area, and add a seat and driver.

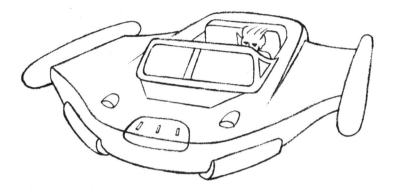

5 Add further details to the cylinder engines, as well as the area immediately in front of the windshield. Draw in a thin rectangle directly behind the seat.

6 To finish your Shuttle Speeder, shade along the bottom of the vehicle. Darken the top of the windshield and along the engine and seat. Sketch in fiery exhaust streams, zooming your Shuttle Speeder across the miles!

The Alien Merchant buys and sells its wares around the galaxy, keeping the most valuable trinkets for its own.

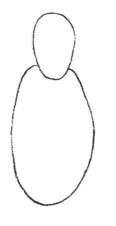

1 Begin this interesting creature with a small egg shape for the head overlapping a larger shape for the body.

2 Guidelines aren't needed here, as you draw in four thick odd-shaped limbs. Make sure its left arm is shaped like a backward "L," as it will be holding a large cane.

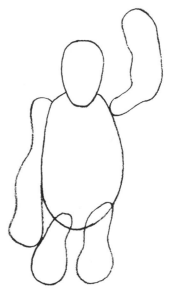

3 Begin to add facial details—an eye, nose, and mouth—along with a turban that has a small circle for an eyehole. Connect the left arm to the body with a small line for the shoulder. Sketch in the fingers and thumb of the left hand, as well as the knuckles of the right. Add two large flat three-toed feet, which have trekked across a better portion of the Milky Way galaxy.

4 In this step, you will add clothing to the Alien Merchant, including a vest, arm and wrist bands (on his right arm), pants, and a low-riding belt. Also suggest a sleeveless T-shirt by adding a V-neck collar. Continue to detail its face with age lines around the eye and nose, as well as further detail to the turban and eyehole, which magnifies everything so the merchant can see the true value of its wares. Sketch in a large pointed ear and small toenails, and erase unneeded lines around its legs and feet. Draw in the merchant's only possessions: a large crooked cane and a heavy canvas bag.

5 Now that you have the basic outline and clothing for your creature, add detail, beginning with the decorative necklace and hooped earrings. Fill in the belt and the arm and wrist bands. Add patches of hair on the forearms, and a left thumbnail, too. Detail the bag and cane. Begin to add ornamentation to the vest.

6 Your creature is almost finished. All that needs to be done is to shade in the bag, cane, and under the arms, pant legs, and feet as shown. Finish detailing its vest.

HEAVY-HEADED HUMANOID

The Heavy-Headed Humanoid is a loyal and trustworthy friend to those who prove themselves worthy. He is the perfect companion for space travel, as he's not over-talkative and has a great love for adventure.

1 To create the Heavy-Headed Humanoid, first draw an odd oval shape for the head. Below that, add an inverted conical shape to outline his shoulders and narrow waist. Establish the pose of the character with guidelines for the legs, neck, hips, and arms, which should be bent at the elbow. Add in simple box shapes for the hands, and indicate with lines where the feet will be placed.

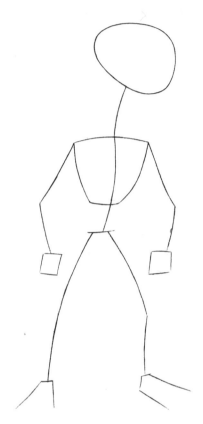

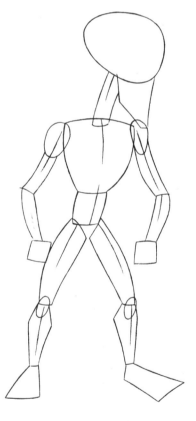

2 Now focus on filling out the creature's body. Sketch in rounded lines on either side of the guidelines on the neck, arms, hips, legs, and feet. Add small oval shapes to show where the shoulders and knees are. From the humanoid's head, add a small jutting shape to indicate his mouth and pointy jaw.

Drawing Tip: To give the illusion of shiny black clothing, fill in the center of the clothes with dark shading, and leave the edges white, as seen on the next page with the gloves, pants, and sandals.

3 Begin to detail the facial features as shown. Define the chest area, too, with simple curving lines. Accentuate the waist with a small belt. Add two curved spikes that protrude from his spine and are used for protection. Erase unneeded lines in the shoulders, neck, arms, legs, torso, and knees. Small rectangular fingers and toes extend from the hand and foot blocks. Don't forget the thumbs!

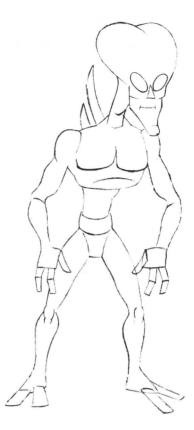

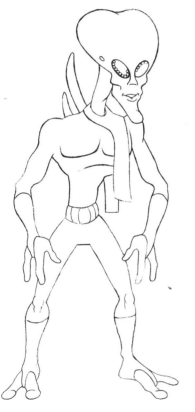

4 Continue to add details, especially around the face. Don't forget to add the small earhole. Add a draping neckpiece around the creature's neck and over his left shoulder. Other clothing items are fingerless gloves for the forearms and calf-high sandals for the feet. Fill in details around the belt. Erase all extra lines in the toes, hands, head, and torso area.

5 To complete the Heavy-Headed Humanoid, finish filling in the eyes, mouth, and ear hole. Shade in details on the clothing, as well as on the spikes. To accentuate the cheek, chin, chest, knuckles, and toes, add extra-dark shading.

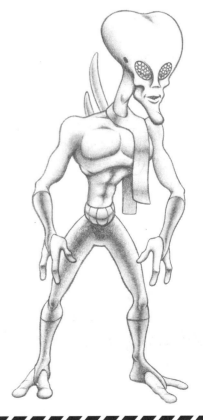

STARSHIP COMMANDER

The Starship Commander, who has cruised space most of his life, learning and training on the Space Station, hopes one day to reach the ultimate goal—to be the captain of his own ship.

1 Draw the basic outline of the Starship Commander by first sketching in an oval-shaped head, then, underneath it, drawing in a square-shaped torso. Add guidelines for the neck, legs, and arms, with his right arm bent at the elbow. Add in small cross lines at the knees and left elbow. Then draw in the feet and hand shapes.

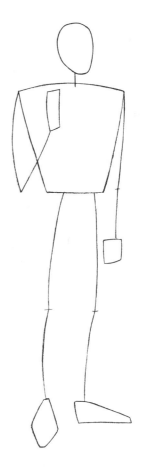

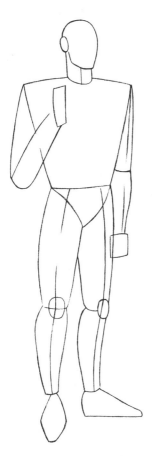

2 Begin to fill out the body of the commander, sketching in arm shapes, leg shapes, a neck, and a small triangular pelvis. Add two small ovals over the cross lines for the knees, and a small oval on the right side of his head for the ear.

Drawing Tip: The first two steps in this drawing will form a basic body shape—any body shape. This can be used as a jumping-off point to create your very own spaceship commander, with his or her own kind of clothing and unique style!

3 Draw in facial details, including eyes, eyebrows, a nose, and a mouth. Add hair as shown, as well as a simple cap. Dress your Starship Commander in a futuristic uniform, giving the short coat a zipper down the middle and bands around the wrists, waist, and neck. Add pants and details to the boots. Begin to erase all the unneeded lines in the arms and legs. Don't forget to suggest the high-powered viewscope, which the commander holds in his right hand.

4 Continue to detail his uniform with several small lines around his wrists, waist, and neck, and a few wider stripes down his pants and sleeves. Add zippers to his boots. Further detail the commander's face, right hand, and binoculars, and sketch in a headset, complete with a mouthpiece and ear antenna. Also draw in a stun gun and waist pouches, and suggest military stripes on his chest.

5 Detail all of the commander's equipment, including the ear antenna, viewscope, stun gun, and waist pouches. Then further decorate and shade his uniform with more detail on his military stripes, the stripes down his chest and pant legs, and the planet logo on his right arm (which partially shows on his left arm) and his cap. Shade in his boots, hair, and around his clothing as shown.

The dangerous Insect Viper evolved over millions of years into the lethal killer it is. Its earliest ancestor? The black ant from planet Earth.

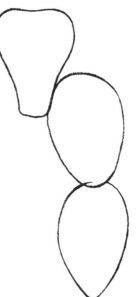

1 Like its Earthly relatives, this creature has three portions to its body: the head (which is almost triangular), thorax, and abdomen.

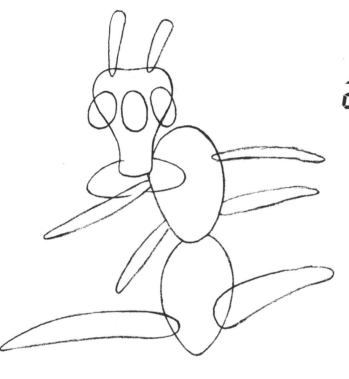

2 Add the beginnings of its six appendages, four connected to the thorax, and two larger shapes connected to, and overlapping, the abdomen. Draw in three ovals for its eyes, which seem to be popping out of its head. Sketch in two antennae, as well as two good-sized jaws around its mouth area.

3 Add a foreleg section to each of the six appendages (the additions to the lowest legs should be ribbed on the inside). Then add three additional segments to each of the antennae. Sketch in three small sensory holes above the eyes. Connect the head to the upper body with a small thin neck. Create four pincers on the upper appendages, and complete the large jaw. Add detail to the snout as shown. Finally, sketch in three lines at the base of the abdomen.

4 Once you add the two long-toed feet, you have finished the outline of your creature. Add a leg band around its lower right leg and a wrist band around its upper left arm. Continue to add detail to the snout and antennae. Sketch in a small crescent-moon shape at the top of its abdomen. Add its alien weapon, held by its upper left and right arms.

5 The key to finishing your Insect Viper is to shade, shade, shade. Use darker shading around the lower edges of the limbs and outer edges of the body, and lighter shading inside the body and limbs. Notice the particular shading in the eyes: a thin white outline with a darker center toward the bottom of the eye.

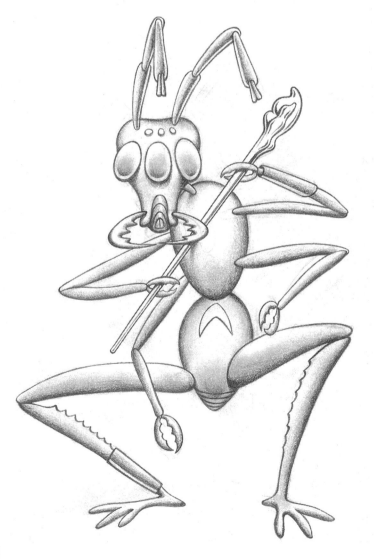

CYBERSPACE STARSHIP CRUISER

The Cyberspace Starship Cruiser is the largest spaceship ever developed. Traveling at light speed across the universe, this carrier can haul thousands of passengers at a time.

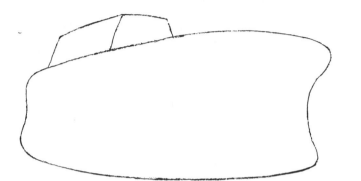

1 Start your ship by drawing a large horizontal oblong shape, with two curved indentations on either side. Add a small box shape at the top rear end for the bridge crew.

2 Sketch in a curved line on top of the bridge. This is the watch cabin. Add a center engine: a horizontal oval shape overlapping the ship's body. Then draw a smaller oval inside the oval you just drew. Indicate the side wing shapes on either side of the cruiser.

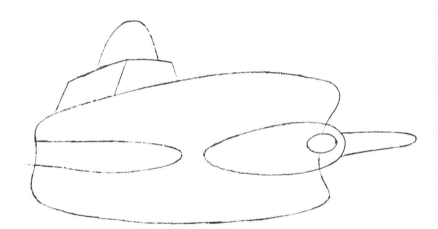

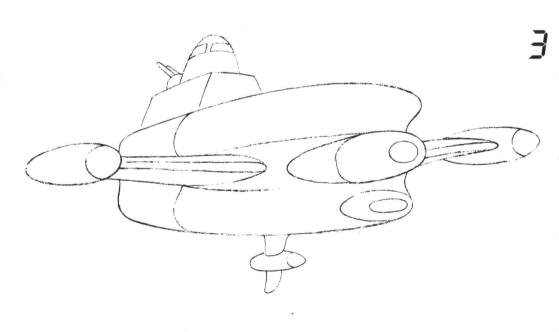

3 Complete the wings by adding flattened oval shapes on either side for two more engines. Sketch in a curved line at the front end of the three engines. Add a lower window area directly beneath the center engine—it should be a small flattened oval inside a larger oval. Draw a small fin shape connecting another engine to the bottom of the cruiser. Add additional lines on the large ship's body and wings. Detail the watch cabin with windows, and add rear guns.

4 Now that you've constructed the entire ship's body, wings, and engines, you can add detail throughout. Draw small rectangular windows in each main segment as shown. Continue to add contour lines to the main body, and add small vertical lines to the window below the center engine.

5 In this final step, you will add finishing touches all over your Cyberspace Starship Cruiser. Thicken lines around the entire ship, especially on the front of the carrier and center engine. Shade around the underside of the ship, on the engine fin, and on the wings. Fill in the rear gun carrier. With a thin pencil, add fiery exhaust blasts from the side and bottom engines.

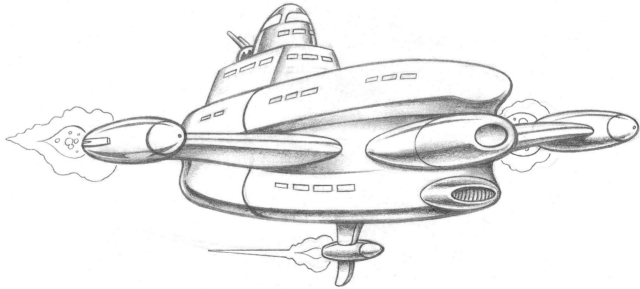

This victim of several failed genetic experiments lurks around sewers of cyberspace cities. It may look horribly menacing, but it's actually pretty harmless.

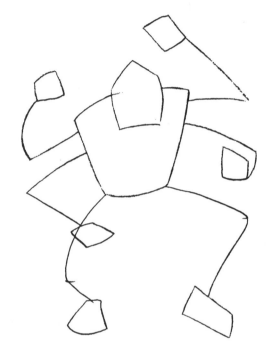

1 Draw a loose pentagon shape for the mutant's head, overlapping a four-sided shape for its body. Add six guidelines for its limbs: four arms and two legs. The small shapes on the end of each limb are the beginnings of the hands and feet. Sketch in cross lines at the knees, and erase the unneeded line in the head.

2 Begin to fill out the mutant by sketching around the two upper arms and the legs. Add clawlike fingers to all the hands, and draw in pointed toes—five on one foot, four on the other. Start to detail the face with one large eye, a half-closed eye, nostrils, and a wide mouth. Don't forget to add the two oversized ears and sharp horn. Sketch in chest lines and a small oval for the right knee.

3 Continue creating your mutant by filling in the second pair of arms now. Add further detail to the face, especially the mouth, which should have two thick lips. Draw in a torn pair of crusty pants with a huge rip on the upper left leg. Add another line on the chest, and erase unneeded lines around the hands, feet, and arms. On the mutant's upper right forearm and left ankle, sketch in skin fins, which come in handy for swimming in sewage!

4 Add two more sets of skin fins on the second set of forearms. Add a hastily sewn scar on its forehead, a belly button on its stomach, and a rope around its pants. Begin to show texture with small bumps on its right shoulder, arm, and chest. Erase all extra lines around the pants, arms, and chest.

5 Finally, bring this creature to life by shading around its arms, feet, and chest, and add more bumpy warts on its body. Darken the undersides of the pant legs to suggest shadows, and add more detail to the rope belt.

WINGED ALIEN

This basically intelligent but menacing carnivorous creature prefers to travel in flocks—by land or sea, or even through the vacuum of space!

1 First draw a curving "S" shape for the outer contour of the alien's body. Add a triangular shape for the head on the upper end of the curved line. Then sketch in two upside-down "V" shapes on either side of the top rounded "hump" of the curved line.

2 Finish drawing the base of the wings. To the tops of the wings, add small squares that will be the "hands" to which you'll be adding claws. Sketch a second curved line to thicken the body, gradually thinning the body from the lower jaw down to the pointy tail. Begin to add facial details with eyes and a rounded line for the upper jaw.

3 Add small rectangles and triangles to create the long claws. Begin to add details to the fleshy wings. As for the body, sketch in a third curved line in between the first two. This will indicate the underbelly area. Add nostrils, then line the inside of the lower jaw.

4 Draw several horizontal lines down the front of the body to suggest scales in the underbelly. Add an arsenal of sharp jagged teeth, as well as the short but deadly spikes down the back of its neck. Begin to add texture to the top side of the Winged Alien, starting at the tail and working up.

5 Finish adding short texture lines up its body and around its snout and eyes. Darken its mouth as needed, and shade around the body, wings, and claws as shown. Pay special attention to the bottom of the creature, where it gets darker and has a thicker outline.

GALACTIC EMPEROR

This evil slug is one of the nastiest rulers of the galaxy. For an emperor, he's really rather slow—physically *and* mentally!

1 Sketch in a large head shape overlapping an even bigger oblong shape for the body. Add two small square shapes at a slight angle for the hands.

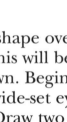 **2** Draw a small oval shape overlapping the top of the head. This will be the base of the emperor's crown. Begin to add facial features with two wide-set eyes and a large drooping mouth. Draw two curved lines on either side of the Galactic Emperor to form fat arms. Add thumbs, and indicate the fingers with small lines on the hand shapes. Erase the extra line inside the base of the crown.

3 Sketch in the top part of the crown with two triangle shapes next to each other and three small circles for jewels at the two points and bottom center. Add two small bumps on either side of the mouth, above the chin. Begin to add clothing to the creature with a furlike material around his neck and shoulders, and folds of satin around his arms.

4 Finish dressing the ruler by draping his robe down to the ground. At his neckline, indicate the robe and attach a royal pin to keep the robe in place. Add a small pointed shape in the crown to complete his headpiece. Put a scepter in the Galactic Emperor's hands, and erase all unnecessary lines in the robe. Start to add detail to the robe, beginning with the emperor's right sleeve, and indicate texture to the crown with tiny dark circles drawn side by side. At this time, you can also begin to sketch in texture on the ruler's bumpy, rough skin with small circles and curved lines.

5 Continue to detail your creature with scaly skin bumps on his face, arms, and body, particularly around the lowest portion of his body. Finish adding decoration to the robe and crown. Lightly shade in the fur around his shoulders, and fill in areas around the mouth and eyes for added definition. With smooth-tone shading, darken sections around the crown, scepter, and robe. Last, darken the areas underneath his body and arms.

Cargo ships and research vessels, aliens and humans—they all pass through the Space Station in their journeys through the galaxy. Some come to get repairs made on their starships; others meet to chat over a cup of superb hyperspace cappuccino.

1 First draw three wide ovals, the largest resting at an angle under the other smaller two.

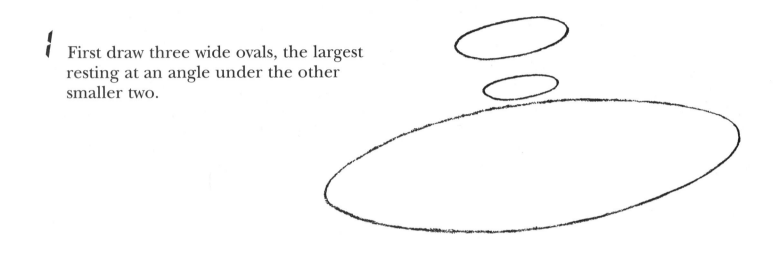

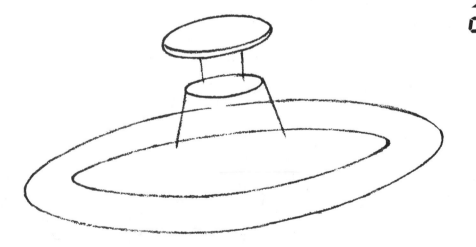

2 Add another slightly smaller oval inside the largest oval of the Space Station, creating a ring. Sketch a narrow parallel line around the bottom curve of the topmost oval to give this section a three-dimensional disk shape. Add two small vertical lines near the center of the top disk, running down to the middle oval. Then draw two straight, slanting lines from the middle disk to the ring at the bottom.

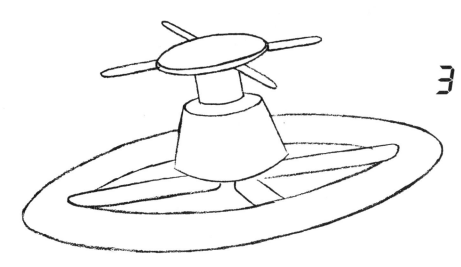

3 Now draw four thin tubelike cylinders branching out from the topmost disk. Add curved lines to create two wide cylinders—one that sits at the center of the ring, and one that rests on top of that. Add three wide cylinder shapes, for spokes, branching inside the large ring area.

4 Extend a thick cylinder down from beneath the large body, then sketch in three thinner cylinders extending from the thick one. Now add the small basic shapes to form a spaceship flying toward the station.

5 Now your Space Station is ready for detailing. Add metal seamwork here and there, as well as small rectangular windows as shown. Be sure to give the horizontal lines on the ring's windows a slight curve so that they seem to follow the ring's curved contours. Then give the spaceship two small windows, side engines, and a tail fin, and begin to add exhaust lines.

6 Add smooth shading around the lower area of the large ring, and wherever else is needed to give the Space Station a sleek, finished look. Darken the upper portions of all the windows, while highlighting the lower portions. Add long swerving exhaust lines to show how the spaceship is making a tight turn into the Space Station.

Cybil is half-human, half-robot. She works for a mysterious organization whose name no one knows. Her job? Those secret missions that no one else dares try. And she's never failed . . . at least not yet.

1 Begin creating your own cyborg agent by drawing the outline of her body. First draw her oval-shaped head. Then create the outline of her chest. Attach the head and body with a thin skeletal line for the neck. Draw thin lines for the arms and the legs, including cross lines at the knees and elbows. Sketch in small shapes for the hands and feet, making sure that her feet are pointed at the ends.

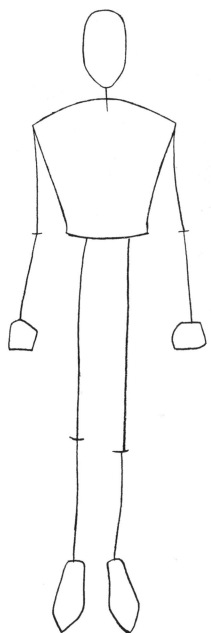

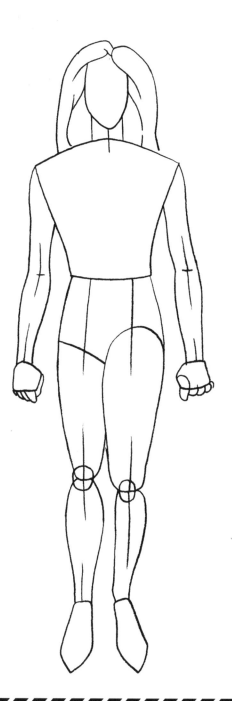

2 Cybil has long hair, which you can add by drawing curvy lines that reach down to her shoulders. Based on the guidelines, fill out her neck, arms, and legs, and below her torso, add a pelvis area. Then add knuckles to her hands. Sketch in small circles at the knee joints.

3 Start adding facial features, with one human eye, one robotic eye, a nose, and mouth. Don't forget her ears. Her shirt should be pointed at her shoulders. On both of her arms add mechanical devices. Notice that her left hand is robotic, while the right is human. On her left leg, give the agent long shorts. The clothing on her right side extends slightly beyond her shirt. Create a metal bar that extends from the top of the right leg to the circular hinge at the knee. Be sure to add metal bands on the lower part of this leg as well as the metal points at her toes. Erase all your guidelines.

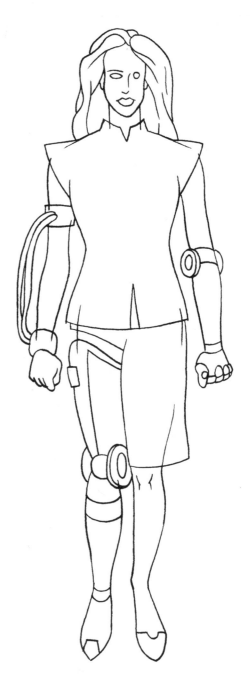

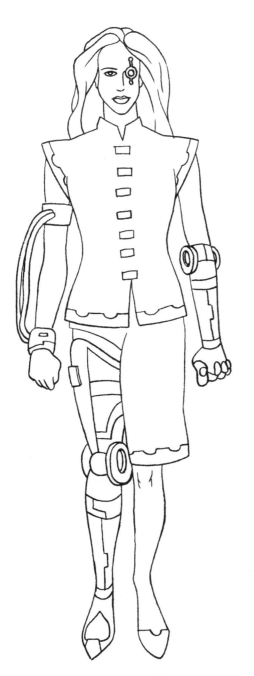

4 As Cybil is only partially human, continue to add detail to the robotic body parts to make them look like they're completely formed from metal plates. Pay particular attention to her left arm, right leg, and left eye. Add lips to her mouth, and fill in her human eye. Add buttons and other decorative details to her clothing. Erase any unnecessary lines.

5 Cybil is nearly ready to take on the galaxy's criminal element. First darkly shade along her metal leg and other robotic sections, leaving some areas highlighted. Shade her clothing as shown. Also shade underneath her hair and wherever else is needed.

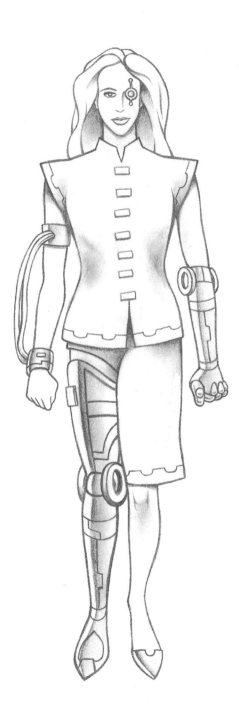

Drawing Tip: Using the basic form of this cyborg agent, you can create your own personal secret spy by drawing in different clothes, facial features, and even varied robotic parts!

SPACE PIRATE

With its swordlike arm, robotic strength, and savage nature, there is none more feared in all the galaxy (and beyond) than the dreaded Space Pirate.

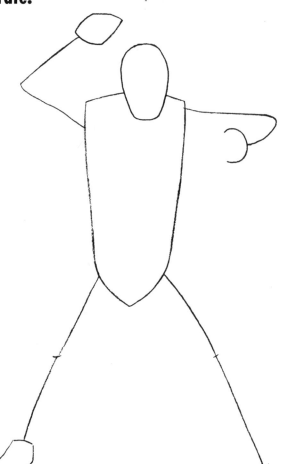

1 Begin your drawing with a basic oval head overlapping an elongated rectangular torso shape, slightly pointed on the end. Draw guidelines to show the length and position of the limbs, with the right arm raised just over the head. Add small block shapes for the right hand and right foot. Suggest a left hand with a backward "C" shape and small cross lines for the knees and the bottom left leg, which will become a peg leg.

2 Now you're ready to fill out your Space Pirate. Beginning with the right arm, add a billowy sleeve on the upper arm, as well as an outline of the robotic wrist and hand. Suggest a blouse on the left arm as well, and include a sharp deadly sword for the left wrist and hand. Next sketch in the lower portion of your pirate's body, giving it a large thigh-length boot on its right leg and a knee-high peg leg on its left. Now put a metal cap over this creepy creature's skull and left eye. Add one large eye, a small hole for its nose, and a "U" shape extending just below the face for its lower jaw. Sketch in more clothing details, including a wide sash around the pirate's waist, a square-shaped collar around its neck, a large drape over its right shoulder, and a small capped sleeve on its left shoulder.

3 Erase all the guidelines. Continue to add detail to the Space Pirate with two metal cables on its right forearm and two small buttons on its right sleeve. Add large, ill-fitting teeth in its upper jaw as shown. Every pirate always keeps a spare weapon handy, and this pirate is no exception. Draw in a space knife attached to its left thigh with two thin bands. On its chest, add two lines going down the center and a half-circle below the belt. You'll soon add intricate detail to this center area. Sketch in folds in the drape, and add a short line in the sword to give it a contoured three-dimensional look. Add a slight heel to the left boot.

4 In this final step, you'll make the Space Pirate look even more fearsome by adding several details. First add intricate curvy lines in the center of its chest plate, zigzag lines on its left capped sleeve, and wider horizontal lines on the drape. Sketch in vertical lines on its left thigh, add a zipper on its right thigh, and detail the right boot with odd shapes. Add short lines up and down every finger and thin, faint diagonal lines through the sword as shown (these are reflection lines). Create an outline inside the square collar. Now you are ready to shade your creature for an even more true-to-life look. Pay close attention to shading on the inner sides of the legs, as well as along the drape and around and under the collar. Fill in the nose and eye sockets.

BRINGING YOUR ALIEN TO LIFE

Here are more tips on how to put life into your drawings. Keep in mind that the most realistic drawings combine several finishing techniques. You can practice and experiment with your own favorite combinations!

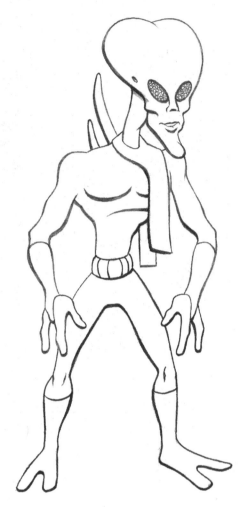

TRY CONTOUR DRAWING

Even if you don't plan to fill in your drawing with color or texture, you can make your space creatures (and spaceships) look more solid by changing the darkness and width of their outlines. For example, note the difference in line weight within the drawing of the Heavy-Headed Humanoid. The lower edges of the figure are thicker and the upper outline is thinner, making the alien look as if it will leap right off the page!

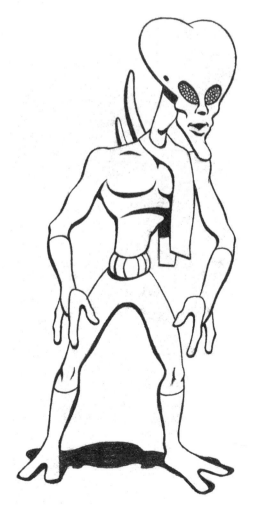

TRY CASTING SHADOWS

Your drawings will look much more realistic if a surface is added for the aliens to stand on. If your creature is standing on a hard surface, as this Heavy-Headed Humanoid is, imagine what kind of shadow it might cast on the ground if light were shining on it from above. Draw the shadow as a dark shape, making it thinner under narrow body parts and fatter under wider body parts. Remember that shadows can not only appear on the ground, but also on the underside of creatures, too, as with the humanoid's drape.

**TRY PLACING A LIGHT FIGURE
AGAINST A DARK BACKGROUND**

You'll be surprised by how rounded your creature or spacecraft will look if you simply darken the space behind it. By filling in the space behind this Heavy-Headed Humanoid, you can create a rounded three-dimensional effect. You can imagine the alien standing at the edge of a galaxy or against the darkness of a galactic cave. Of course, if you add texture to the figure, the effect is even stronger—as with the light hatching on this alien!

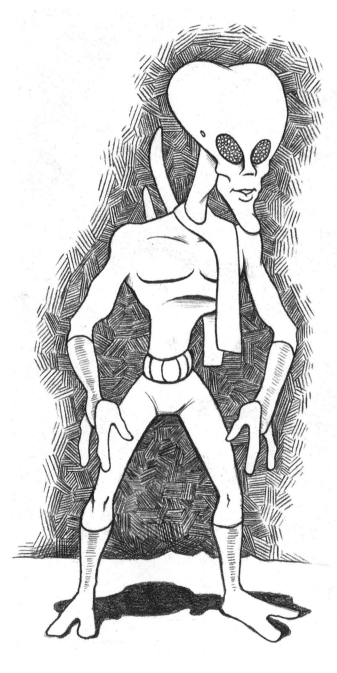

How do you make an alien in a small drawing seem larger? Or a creature in a huge picture seem smaller? The following techniques will show you how.

THE HORIZON LINE

To show how big your creature is in a drawing, add a ground line or horizon line across your picture. If the top of the space creature in your picture is much higher than the horizon line you drew—as with the Heavy-Headed Humanoid on the right—the creature will appear large to the viewer. If the horizon line is near the top of the page and the creature is drawn below the horizon line, the space alien will appear smaller.

ADDING OBJECTS FOR SCALE

Another way to indicate your alien's or spaceship's size is to include objects whose size most people know. People know that coins, for instance, are small. Drawing them almost as wide as an Antigravity Servo-Robot indicates the small size of the robot. Conversely, if you draw a robot trying to fit on top of a planet, the viewer will see your Antigravity Servo-Robot as gigantic! For fun, try adding an Earthling to your drawings to give observers an instant idea of the size of your figures.

POINT OF VIEW

You can also show the approximate size of an alien by drawing it from a certain perspective. If you were flying through the atmosphere over a small unnamed planet, you could see space creatures from almost any angle. If you saw a Canine Creature below you, it would seem smaller than you. On the other hand, if you were looking at its belly from underneath, it would seem larger. By drawing your creature from either of these perspectives, you can give an impression of its size.

BACKGROUNDS

Once you have completed a drawing, you may want to put your creature or vehicle in a setting. For many of your illustrations, the background can be outer space, but you can add all sorts of things to make the scenery interesting. Use your imagination! Here are some suggestions for creating different settings.

MAGAZINE BACKGROUNDS

If you like to cut and paste, ask your family for some old magazines you can cut up. Cut out pictures of different patterns and trim them so they're shaped like craters, rocks, a cave, or even an alien cityscape. This will give your picture an interesting abstract look. And you don't have to fill the entire page. A few groupings to the side or below your main drawing will give the impression of a whole scene.

PAINTED BACKGROUNDS

You don't need a paintbrush to add painted backgrounds! To create small craters on a planet's surface, dip the end of a drinking straw into some paint and print tiny indentation pockets around your alien. You can make smaller craters by using the ends of tiny macaroni, or bigger ones with large macaroni. Cut a piece of sponge, dip it in paint, and stamp it on your picture to create a rock texture. A crumpled piece of waxed paper or a paper towel can achieve the same effect. Be sure not to get these too wet, though, or they won't work well. Look around the house for other printing tools, such as old wooden spools, corrugated cardboard, or cut pieces of Styrofoam.

TEXTURED BACKGROUNDS

If you want to create a textured background, you'll need to draw your space alien or vehicle on a thin piece of paper. Place a textured object (such as sandpaper) under the section of your paper where you want the texture to appear. Now grab a pencil with a soft lead. Then, using the side of the pencil lead, rub lightly and evenly over the area. For other cool textures, try using window screening, rough wood, a kitchen grater—anything you can imagine!

SHADOWED BACKGROUNDS

By adding shadows in the right places, your illustrations will leap off the page! Imagine where the shadow of your alien or vehicle would fall underneath itself. Then fill in those areas with a dark pencil. You might want to add shadows to some of the rocks or background scenery, too. When adding shadows to your backgrounds, remember that sunlight is different at different times of the day. Morning and late afternoon light makes objects cast very long shadows. Whenever the sun is directly overhead, the shadows cast are very short.

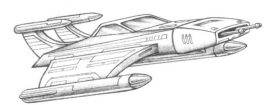

Your picture will stand out from the rest of the crowd if you use these helpful tips on how to add color to your masterpiece!

TRY WHITE ON BLACK

For a different look, try working on black construction paper or art paper. Then instead of pencil, use white chalk, white prismacolor pencil, or poster paint. With this technique, you'll need to concentrate on drawing the light areas in your picture rather than the dark ones. Because space is inky black, this technique is just right for drawing your aliens or vehicles to give them an authentic-looking space background.

TRY BLACK AND WHITE ON GRAY (OR TAN)

You don't need special gray or tan paper from the art store for this technique. Instead, try cutting apart the inside of a grocery bag or a cereal box. This time, your background is a middle tone (neither light nor dark). Sketch your drawing in black, then use white to make highlights. Add black for the shadows. Don't completely cover up the tan or gray of the cardboard. Let it be the middle tone within your illustration. With this technique, your pictures can have a very finished look with a minimal amount of drawing!

TRY COLOR

Instead of using every color in your marker set or your colored pencil set, try drawing in black for shadows, white for highlights, and one color for a middle tone. This third color blended with the white creates a fourth color. You will be surprised how professional your drawing will look.

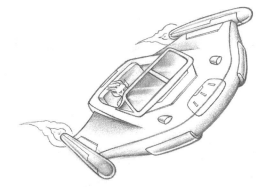

You've drawn crazed mutants, galactic warriors, servo-robots, and all sorts of space vehicles, but don't let your sci-fi journey end just yet! The best aliens and space transporters are yet to be drawn, for those are the pictures that you create in your mind.

Take the drawing tips and suggestions that you've learned throughout this book to help get you started developing your very own universe. You may want to use the basic foundations for some of the characters shown here and use your imagination to alter them in your own distinctive style.

Explore what a city would look like in your future galaxy. How would a school be structured? A playground? You can even create your own personal robot assistant, custom designed to fit your specific desires.

Have fun, and keep your pencils sharp and your eyes on the stars!